Venus H

John McGreevey

Alpha Editions

This edition published in 2024

ISBN : 9789362929457

Design and Setting By
Alpha Editions
www.alphaedis.com
Email - info@alphaedis.com

As per information held with us this book is in Public Domain. This book is a reproduction of an important historical work. Alpha Editions uses the best technology to reproduce historical work in the same manner it was first published to preserve its original nature. Any marks or number seen are left intentionally to preserve its true form.

VENUS HATE

By JOHN McGREEVEY

She was joy. She was death. She was part of the Desert Rouge—and the desert blotted out her sins.

When the patrol found her it was impossible to say how long she had been in the humidi-hut alone. She was incoherent but, as Morrissey observed, most Venusians are.

Not that Selo was an ordinary Venusian woman. Even in her madness, as she babbled to the patrol about red dust devils and punctured thermiteens, there was a haunting beauty about her. Those deep-set violet eyes, the blue-black hair, the shapely, well-rounded body—easy to understand why an earthman might be hypnotized by such a woman.

At first she was passive. Their questions made no impression upon her. She nodded her head absently and gestured vaguely toward the vac-lock that led to the dust-tortured world outside. Once or twice, Morrissey thought he heard her mutter Yancey's name but he couldn't be sure. Her speech was a confused mixture of English and the indecipherable polyglot of Venus.

The simplest solution seemed to be to take Selo back to Athens where technicians could subdue her hysteria and perhaps eventually draw the whole tragic story from her paralyzed mind.

Morrissey wouldn't have admitted it to any of the members of his patrol, but he found the woman's manner disconcerting. She stared at the vac-lock as though she momentarily expected Yancey to appear there. So intense was the stare that if Morrissey hadn't seen Yancey Ritter's desiccated body himself, he could have believed that the woman had second sight.

Her passivity was abruptly shattered when they tried to get ready for the trip. She clawed and bit like a mad animal as they struggled to slip the plasti-shield over her shoulders.

"Let me die as Brian died!" she wailed. "I do not want to live without him. You cannot make me live."

"Hey, captain," a panting patrolman shouted, "what do we do with her?"

"Put that plasti-shield on her. Tie it if you have to. She's not to go through that vac-lock without it."

The frenzy that had seized Selo seemed to subside as quickly as it began. She permitted them to make the plasti-shield secure. Her face, through the greenish-gray mask, had the texture and shading of a corpse. Zombie-like, she had lost all individuality.

"Check your thermiteens," Morrissey snapped to the patrol, "and let's get out of this place."

The men quickly filled their light-weight thermiteens with water from the supply in the humidi-hut, fastened their own plasti-shields securely over head and shoulders, put on their asbesti-mittens and stepped into the vac-lock.

Sixty seconds later, the party stood in the weird, dust-filled world outside. A hot wind pressed its dusty fingers against their protective hoods and tugged with an eerie persuasiveness at their padded jackets. Through the murk an orange sun burned in the sand-strewn sky. Rocks pitted and pocked from centuries of relentless persecution stood stark sentinel on every side. This was Venus.

Walking slightly behind Selo, shoulders hunched, head down, Morrissey worried the enigma of this strange Venusian woman and the two men who had known her. Two men—now both dead—wind-dried mummies fallen in the wastes of the Desert Rouge.

Victims of the desert, Morrissey wondered, or victims of a woman with deep-set violet eyes and blue-black hair.

The Earth colonies on Venus, Mars and the satellites of Jupiter are filled with men like Yancey Ritter. They're men who seem to be born with a weight of bitterness on their backs. They look at the Universe early in life and decide that things are set against them—that they are the persecuted and misunderstood. You've heard them talking in bars.

"If I just had a chance I'd make it. I just never get the breaks."

Yancey Ritter said that a thousand times in his life. He said it when he was prospecting for brakion on Mars, when he tried lumbering on

Europa, and finally, when he took the assignment to the humidi-hut on Venus.

That job, of course, was to be only a stepping stone. When Yancey wasn't preoccupied with the relatively simple routine of maintaining the humidi-hut he planned to search for quollas. The edge of the Desert Rouge, near the humidi-hut to which Yancey had been assigned, was reputed to be an ideal locale for such a search.

The quolla, an amazingly beautiful gem burnished to a glowing loveliness by the wind and sand, brought an increasingly fancy price in the jewel markets of the System. A few sizeable finds and Yancey would have a little capital with which to work. Given fifty thousand credits he was certain that he could, in time, become one of the really big investors on Venus.

Such projects always assumed a false simplicity in Yancey's mind. Aboard the space tramp that brought him to Athens his sudden rise to power and position seemed quite feasible. But when he gazed out across the tortured wastes of the Desert Rouge he felt a momentary tremor of doubt.

Such spasms passed quickly. Like most men of his temperament Yancey compensated for the failures of past and present with roseate dreams of the future. Now, it appeared, that future was at hand.

The commandant in Athens was brutally frank.

"It would appear to me, Ritter," he said wryly, "that tenacity is not one of your cardinal virtues."

Yancey cleared his throat. He was trying hard not to be impressed by the commandant's office, the commandant's ribbons, the commandant's manner. "I don't know what you mean, sir."

The big man tapped the papers on his desk with a stubby finger. "Governmental service on Earth ... mining on Mars ... lumbering on Europa ... and now, an assignment on Venus. Not the record of a stable personality."

Yancey was bewildered. What was the commandant saying? Wasn't he to get the post? The dream of a fortune in quollas flickered. "I—I've been looking for work that would really challenge me, sir."

The gaze was direct. "Challenge you. That's an interesting answer, Ritter. So you think that assignment to a humidi-hut in the vicinity of the Desert Rouge will awaken your latent and heretofore unexplored potentials?"

Was the man laughing at him? Even in the carefully conditioned room, Yancey felt the beads of perspiration settling on his forehead. "If I was just given a chance," he said, seizing on the familiar cliche. "I know I can please the commandant."

A sigh escaped the big man. "Pleasing me is irrelevant. Keeping that humidi-hut operating is vital. Do you realize, Ritter, that since we established our chain of humidi-huts on Venus we've reduced our mortality rate thirty per cent?"

A nod seemed to be all that was required from Yancey.

"I just want you to realize that the job you're taking can't be abandoned one fine morning when you're seized with a whim to go to Saturn."

"I tell you, sir, I think I've found what I want here. You needn't have no worries about me leaving the service." Yancey felt better. He was back on solid ground. The old man was afraid he'd leave without notice. They were all alike. No matter where you went—Earth, Mars, Europa, Venus—employers were always worried about being left in a spot.

"Human lives depended upon your efficiency, Ritter. Earthmen can only endure so much of this Venusian heat and dust, then we dehydrate. It's up to you to see to it that your station is always alert to the needs of any one in your sector."

Words—only words. Yancey's mind was far away, searching the dust of the Desert Rouge for the beautiful quolla stones.

"You'll be paid three hundred credits a month and living expenses. I might add, Ritter, that the station you're getting is one of the most important in the entire chain."

Three hundred credits! And, with a little luck, Yancey thought, he could find quollas worth a hundred times as much.

"There'll be a patrol to escort you to the station and I think you'd better plan to leave at once." There was a small pause as the commandant regarded Yancey closely. "I hope," he said at last, "that neither of us is making a mistake, Ritter."

Yancey stood up, shook hands with the commandant, and the interview was ended.

Morrissey headed the patrol which escorted Yancey to his new post. Yancey took an almost immediate dislike to the broad-shouldered young space militiaman. There was about Morrissey that air of quiet positiveness which Yancey found impossible to bear.

Throughout the long and tiresome march from Athens to the humidi-hut this unreasoning resentment of Morrissey grew. The yielding, insubstantial dust underfoot, the eye-watering furnace glare in the sky, the desiccating heat that seemed to dry up the marrow in a man's bones—all this, through some inexplicable subconscious juggling, became Morrissey's fault.

Inside the comparative comfort of the plasti-shield, Yancey Ritter looked at the raw redness that stretched around, above and below him, and wondered what perverse fate had drawn him to this ultimate debacle here on the dust-clouded Desert Rouge. For the first time in his life Yancey knew the bowel-rending terror of utter desolation.

The spectre of thirst hovered in the orange and yellow dust clouds ahead. Crazed rocks, scarred and wind-broken, leered at him like blind prophets wordlessly screaming their dire predictions.

Morrissey was at last forced to take his thermiteen away from him. He sobbed and pleaded for water. He swore that his tongue was swollen with thirst, that his body was dehydrated. He cursed Morrissey ... the desert ... the service ... his own ill fortune. He made his will, he resigned from the service, he called upon God to avenge his death at the sands of the heartless Morrissey. And finally, after two days on the pitiless griddle of the Desert Rouge, he was half-carried through the vac-lock at the humidi-hut.

Only his hatred for Morrissey made him stay. Every instinct told him to return to Athens with the patrol. Let the commandant hire some other fool to stay there in the midst of the desert, supplying succor for those who were stupid enough to face the rigors of the hell outside. Instinct warned him to leave but hatred forced him to stay. The contempt in Morrissey's eyes permitted him no alternative. The patrol left and Yancey stayed in the humidi-hut.

The first few days were a nightmare. He seemed in a waking dream. Hour upon hour he simply sat and stared at the precious machinery that kept temperature and humidity at ideal levels. Every few minutes he would half-run to check the water supply, touch the water to his lips, anxiously work the controls to be certain that nothing had jammed.

Every second was filled with but one preoccupation: What would happen if the machinery failed?

But the machinery performed in its precise and unhurried way, and from its dependability, he began to draw a degree of confidence. He had let the orange hell outside unnerve him. One could almost think that particles of the wind-driven dust had penetrated his mind and prevented its proper functioning.

Why should he be apprehensive? Hadn't everything worked out exactly as he had planned? The job was his. He had the security of three hundred credits a month and a perfect opportunity to search for quolla stones. The superior attitude of that captain—what was his name—Morrissey—had momentarily shaken his resolve. Now, Morrissey was gone. The time for huddling inside was over. The sooner the quolla stones were his, the sooner he could leave the humidi-hut, make the sort of life he had always wanted for himself in Athens.

Yancey didn't take risks. The first few excursions he made from the humidi-hut were within a radius of fifty yards of his headquarters. Gradually, as he became more accustomed to his plasti-shield, to the murk of the world outside, he grew bolder and bolder. He made several trips to replenish the cache of water half-way between the humidi-hut and Athens. He became very clever in establishing landmarks for himself and he found that with practice, his endurance lengthened. He could go much longer without a drink from his thermiteen and the wind no longer drained him of all vitality.

A little more than a month after Morrissey left him at the humidi-hut, Yancey found his first quolla stone. It wasn't a large one, and it was far from perfect, but for Yancey it seemed the good omen he needed. The quolla stones were there to be found. With a little perseverance he could make the rest of his dream come true.

The one inescapable hazard of Yancey's life was the loneliness. Visitors to the station were few, an occasional patrol of space militia, a prospector, or a party of geologists. The days and nights between were long and empty. Yancey would sit polishing the lone quolla stone he had found, wondering if he could stick it out until he had accumulated enough to carry out his long range scheme.

Often, as he groped through the constant veil of orange dust in his search for the gems, he would imagine that there was someone waiting for him at the station, someone to whom he could talk of the difficulties he had faced, someone who could share, perhaps, the dream he held. But, when he passed through the vac-lock, there would be no one—only the monotonous purr of the machinery.

Despite this, when Yancey took the week's leave to visit Athens, he had no idea that he was to meet someone there—that he would not return to the station alone.

You must understand the position of the Venusian women to appreciate the thing that happened with Yancey and Selo.

From the time of the first settlement, fraternization had been frowned upon. No one expected earthmen, twenty-six million miles from home, to ignore the more attractive of the Venusian women. But very few permanent alliances were formed. Militiamen might wink at a buxom beauty, might even invite her caresses to while away a long Venusian night, but with the sunrise she must return to her appointed place in the scheme of things colonial.

Selo was a waitress in one of the cheap Venusian restaurants that dotted the boundary between the old city of Athens and the new. Her uncle, a vicious-looking old fellow with beetling brows, broken nose and protruding teeth, was the proprietor of the place, and, in his unoccupied moments, which were many, he did what he could to make life miserable for the girl.

The moment that Yancey saw her he felt a quickening of his desire. The girl was young. Not more than seventeen or eighteen earth years of age, and despite her wretched clothes she had a distinctive kind of beauty. She lived in constant fear of her uncle, doing her heavy work in the restaurant with the deft but lifeless efficiency of an automaton.

It was apparent to Yancey that it was only a matter of time until someone recognized the girl's potentials and took her away. He could find no reason why he shouldn't be her discoverer.

She was terribly frightened and shy at first. That an earthling should be kind to her seemed beyond her comprehension. Then, once she saw Yancey was serious in his advances, she was certain her uncle would find her out and punish her.

On the fourth night of his visit to Athens, Yancey persuaded Selo to meet him after the restaurant closed. When she slipped furtively out of the shadows to seek haven in his arms he knew that he could not return to the humidi-hut alone. With this woman to care for him he could search for the quollas with new eagerness. She would put an end to the terrible loneliness.

Of course, he told Selo nothing of what he was actually thinking. If he had she would have been much too terrified to understand. He promised to be kind to her and to protect her from any attempt by her uncle to punish her. He told her briefly of the humidi-hut, of the good food, the nice clothes.

In the end, however, it was not so much the good things Yancey promised as the bad things she had suffered which brought Selo to her decision. Life in the restaurant of her uncle had become unbearable. An escape was offered by an earthling. Earthlings very seldom offered Venusian women such security. She promised to go with him.

Yancey was never sure how the commandant learned of his arrangement with Selo. News travels quickly in the Earth Colony at Athens. No doubt the commandant had his spies. Whatever his methods, he knew—and he was displeased.

"I was beginning to think, Ritter," he said, "that I was mistaken—that you were going to serve us well."

Yancey hated the big man for making him feel like a small boy. "I can't see that my taking Selo with me will interfere with my work, sir," he stammered.

The Commandant snorted. "You're making two mistakes. You're aligning yourself with a Venusian. And you're taking a woman to an isolated humidi-hut. I can't order you not to do this, Ritter. You're within your rights. But I am asking you to reconsider." The tone was surprisingly conciliatory.

Yancey shook his head. "I can't go back on my word now, sir. She's counting on it, and frankly, so am I. There won't be no trouble with her, I can promise you that. I'll be able to do an even better job if I'm not so lonely out there."

There was a little pause before the Commandant stood and faced Ritter across the desk. "As I said, I have no authority to forbid your taking the woman with you. I can quite understand that loneliness is a fearful thing. But I've also learned in my stay here, Ritter, that there are other pressures of even greater intensity."

Yancey avoided the calm gray eyes of his superior. "You don't know Selo, sir. She's different."

And on that note the interview was concluded.

On the nightmare trip back to the humidi-hut, Selo was sturdily self-reliant. In fact, on several occasions when the shifting dust made footing insecure, she came to Yancey's assistance. It was Selo who found the auxiliary water cache, one day's journey from the humidi-hut, and led Yancey to it when he had lost the trail. Nature seemed to have equipped Selo for the environmental hazards of the Desert Rouge.

In the early days of their life at the humidi-hut, Yancey worked constantly to convince himself that things were as he had imagined they would be. Certainly Selo was a tireless worker. Her only concern was his comfort. Nonetheless, she was, he decided after two months, a wonderful servant, but no companion.

Her attitude toward Yancey was depressingly similar to that she had toward her uncle, the restaurant owner. This was a strange mixture of respect and fear. And, at times, as he sat alone with her through an endless evening, it came to Yancey that there was also an element of hate.

He found two more small quolla stones, but Selo failed to share his enthusiasm for the gems. She regarded them with a stolid indifference. He remembered that the Venusians placed no value on the stones.

The accumulation of the fortune in quolla stones was not moving at quite the pace he had imagined. The jewels, it appeared, were not to be found in large quantities. They must be painfully searched out in the remotest, most wind-tortured sections of the Desert Rouge.

Succumbing to the usual fit of despondency, Yancey was toying with the notion of abandoning the whole project—returning Selo to Athens and taking a space tramp back to earth—when Brian Daniels stumbled into the humidi-hut.

There had been no visitors in more than three weeks. Daily, Selo's defiant passivity rankled more and more. Having abused her verbally and physically for an hour on that particular day, Yancey had stormed out into the murk and spent a frustrating afternoon in his futile search for quollas.

He staggered back through the veil of red dust, cursing his rotten luck, cursing Selo, cursing Venus and the twisted destiny that had brought him there. Since Venus and destiny were more or less impervious, he had determined to relieve his frustration by beating Selo.

A fine frenzy had been achieved when he stepped through the vac-lock and saw her. She was sitting on the floor with a stranger's head cradled in her lap. The stranger was making light moaning noises and Selo was soothing him with a little crooning sound as she forced water between his blistered lips.

Yancey's fine anger was lost. "Where did he come from?" he growled, towering over Selo and the stranger.

"He is a prospector. He lost his way. Another few hours on the desert and he would die."

Yancey stared down at the stranger. Despite the terribly blistered face, the stubble of a beard, the matted hair, it was apparent that this Earthman was handsome beyond the ordinary. The features were beautifully modeled—eyes set wide apart, generous mouth, firm chin. And, there was also something intangible about the stranger that troubled Yancey. It was an air of quiet self-possession that refused to be denied even while he was in semi-coma. This was a man who had been given by nature all the qualities Yancey Ritter most prized and least possessed.

In the days that followed, Selo never left Brian Daniels' side. It was as if all her life she had waited for someone upon whom she could lavish such care. She nursed him not so much out of his need as out of her own. Yancey's bitter, jealous remarks failed to touch her.

Under such care, Brian recovered quickly and he seemed to find in Selo a something for which he, too, had long sought. In the few days of his convalescence they achieved the sort of communion that Yancey had dreamed of when he had first brought Selo to the humidi-hut.

Yancey's conversations with Brian were brief and charged with hate. Daniels had been prospecting for quolla stones. He was on his way back to Athens and had lost his bearings. Only the humidi-hut had saved him from death. When he spoke to Yancey, he seemed always anxious to return to Selo, a preoccupation that only deepened the seething hatred Yancey had conceived for him.

More than once, Yancey ordered Selo to keep out of Brian's way but it was the same as if no words were spoken. In the unfaltering stare of those deep-set eyes, Yancey read her open defiance. So desperate was her need for Brian that nothing short of death could keep her from him.

Nothing short of death.

Yancey viewed that possibility. Murder in such a remote place would be easy but what was to be gained? Selo certainly wouldn't love him more if he killed the prospector. Another consideration was Daniels' build. He was a well-muscled man and, being fully recovered, was something less than the ideal murder victim.

And then Yancey found out about the quolla stones—quite by accident. He had gone out on a routine check of the vicinity and had turned back earlier than usual. As he stepped through the vac-lock he saw Selo and Brian huddled in earnest conversation. So engrossed were they, they failed to hear the asthmatic wheeze of the lock. Yancey stood a long time silently watching them.

On the table before the two was a glittering pile of the most beautiful quolla stones Yancey had ever seen. Dozens of them. A small fortune lying quietly on that table in the humidi-hut. Here were the black stones that Yancey had dreamed of finding. Here was the answer to all his hopes.

But the answer lay in another man's hands, the hands that now caressed Selo!

"I won't be long in Athens," Brian was saying. "There's at least sixty or seventy thousand credits worth of quolla stones there. I'll take what they'll offer me in the market, Selo, and then I'll come back for you."

The woman pressed closer to Daniels. "Don't leave me here even for a little while—with him."

Brian's arms went around her. "This is the best way, Selo. He'll make trouble. It's not going to be pleasant. Let me get rid of the stones first and then you and I can start out together."

She buried her face in his chest. "I'm so afraid—here alone with him."

Brian tilted her chin up to face him. "There's no reason to be afraid of him. I know his kind. He only talks about things he could do. He won't hurt you. He wouldn't dare."

They were lost in each other's arms as Yancey turned and silently slipped back through the vac-lock. When he noisily re-entered a half hour later his plans were made.

If Brian was surprised by Yancey's sudden change in attitude, he gave no indication. He accepted Yancey's solicitous interest as lightly as he had his surly resentment earlier.

Dinner, the evening before Brian was to set out for Athens, was an hilarious affair on the surface. Yancey insisted on toasting Brian, on exacting a promise that he would come back to visit them. He assured the prospector that they would miss him and that he must consider the humidi-hut his home when he was on Venus.

Brian seemed to accept Yancey's protestations as genuine. Selo regarded her husband with quiet suspicion.

The next morning Yancey made all the preparations for Brian's departure. He had painstakingly drawn a detailed map of the route to Athens. He personally chose a new plasti-shield to protect Brian from the pelting of the dust and sand. Finally he filled the two thermiteens with their precious supply of water.

Finishing up this last chore in the little lab which housed the water supply, he smiled to himself, for he knew that Brian was using his absence from the living-room to pay Selo a fond farewell.

Only as the vac-lock closed on Brian and the indicator showed them he had left the humidi-hut did Yancey relax. He leaned against the door and smiled at Selo.

"So," he half-whispered, "your lover's gone. But he promised you that he'd come back for you, didn't he? Didn't he?"

For a moment Selo met his gaze. Then, she turned and started toward the kitchen.

"I wouldn't leave just yet," he taunted. "I wouldn't leave until you hear why he isn't coming back for you. Doesn't that interest you?"

She stopped, not turning, her back rigid. "I thought you'd change your mind," Yancey went on. "I thought you'd like to know why you can't count on seeing Mr. Brian Daniels again."

He laughed, and the sound was like a bad smell in the close little hut. "The thermiteens are punctured," he giggled. "The water your lover needs is already evaporated. When he wants it, in three or four hours, those thermiteens won't even be moist. He won't be able to keep on to the auxiliary cache. And he won't be able to come back here."

She was moving toward him. "You saw the quollas. You're killing him to get the jewels."

"That's only part of it," he countered savagely. "He deserved to die for many reasons."

With the quick grace of a Martian feline, she started to slip past him to the vac-lock. He caught her arm and twisted it behind her back. She cried out in pain, struggling with a ferocity he hadn't expected. After a moment he succeeded in throwing her to the floor.

"You can't save him," he panted. "Nothing can save him. You're going to sit here with me, Selo, and wait for the desert to kill your lover." Again he laughed. "It won't take long."

All that day and night they watched each other. And the time dragged by, Yancey's excitement increased. Selo, on the other hand, seemed to shrink within herself. It was almost as if in contemplating Brian's death she was dying herself.

Shortly after noon the next day, Yancey set out from the humidi-hut with four thermiteens. Two were full of water and two were empty.

He found Brian's body a little more than an hour's walk from the humidi-hut. Obviously, the prospector had discovered the punctured thermiteens and started back, but the desert moved in for its kill. He had crawled into the shelter of a pile of twisted rock, and with the punctured thermiteens in one hand and the quolla stones in the other, he had died.

Quickly, Yancey substituted the two empty but sound thermiteens he had brought with him for the tell-tale murder-tins. The quolla stones he dropped into the pocket of his asbesticoat.

With a final glance at the shrivelled thing that had once been Brian Daniels, he turned back to the humidi-hut.

He could feel Selo's eyes upon him that evening as he sat polishing the quolla stones. Each time he glanced up from his work she was staring at him.

"Selo," he said at last, continuing his work with the stones, "I hope you're not thinking of revenge."

She made no answer.

"If you ever went to the authorities with your wild story you'd be put in prison for the rest of your life. I'd see to that. No one would take the word of a Venusian against that of an Earthman."

She only stared at the floor.

Carefully, he deposited the gleaming quolla stones in the chamois bag he had bought for just this happy moment.

"Brian Daniels never reached this humidi-hut. Understand? Never reached it. We found him out there, poor fellow, but there was nothing we could do for him. That's the story. Is it clear?"

Her voice seemed to come from a great distance.

"It's clear."

"I'm going to Athens. I'll sell these quolla stones. In good time we'll leave this place. We might even go to another planet. How would you like that, Selo?"

Each word fell with the precision of a stone into water. "That would be very nice."

He rose and walked over to her. "In time, you'll forget him." It was not a positive statement. It was a half-question, as if Yancey were admitting that this was no more than a wish on his part.

Surprisingly, she nodded. "He will be forgotten," she answered.

This was an unexpected victory. It so pleased Yancey that he made her a present of one of the smaller quolla stones as a token of their new understanding.

She was very good to him that night.

Yancey could scarcely wait to be off the following morning. This day would stand out in bold relief against all the gray, futile days of his past. This was the day that would see the beginning of a new and happier life for Yancey Ritter.

Selo helped him make ready and listened with unusual attentiveness to all his instructions. He had his plasti-shield? Yes. The two thermiteens she had filled? Yes. The chamois bag with the quolla stones? Of course.

She permitted him to kiss her and then stood watching as he stepped toward the vac-lock.

Abruptly he turned and stood, hands on his hips, laughing at her. It was a hollow, mirthless, mocking laughter.

"You fool," he roared. "You stupid little fool of a woman. Did you think you could kill ME—Yancey Ritter—with the same trick I used on Daniels? Giving me these punctured thermiteens!" He threw them with a crash at her feet and stepped threateningly toward her.

"Yancey," she cried, and his heavy fist caught her on the side of the head and sent her sprawling to the floor.

"You don't fool me," he said, looking at her. "I'm not a blind fool like Daniels. This is my round to win and I won't be stopped." He turned and strode into the lab for fresh thermiteens.

She was still sprawled in the same spot when he returned. "I'm not finished with you," he snarled. "We'll finish the payment when I get back from Athens."

And with that he disappeared into the vac-lock.

Resolutely, he strode through the flying dust, eyes set on the orange orb that was the sun. A slow steady gait, he had found, was the most practical way to cover distance in the shifting blood dust of the Desert Rouge.

As the morning advanced, the winds that drove the sand seemed to increase in their elemental fury. The sun was all but blotted out and the dust swirled and eddied in an orange and red kaleidescope. It was as if some giant stood and threw great fistfuls of choking sand at Yancey.

He touched the cool water in the thermiteen to his lips often and each time he drank he half-laughed aloud, remembering the disappointment on Selo's face when she saw her trick was discovered.

He skirted wide around the rocks where he had found Brian. No reason to spoil the day by a second glimpse of that grisly sight.

Once or twice it seemed to him that he was being followed but he dismissed the notion as nerves.

Perhaps, he thought, it's Daniels' ghost. And with a harsh laugh he toasted Daniels' ghost in the cool water. He toasted Selo and the commandant and the quolla merchant who would soon give him a fortune for the stones in the chamois bag.

The wind clawed at him with gritty fingers and his boots seemed to sink deeper and deeper into the yielding dust. Every step was an effort and he could feel the slow encroachment of dehydration.

At the auxiliary water cache he promised himself he would use a little of the water to dampen his face.

He finished the last of his water in the thermiteens about nine hours after he had left the humidi-hut. He had drunk more than usual but he decided that his thirst had been aggravated by the storm.

The familiar marker that stood guard over the auxiliary water supply loomed through the shifting murk. He half ran the last few yards, feeling already the soothing coolness of the dampened cloth against his fevered cheek.

He stopped a few paces from the water cache and stared.

The door of the little thermi-safe stood open and there in the drifting dust lay the emptied auxiliary water kegs.

He threw himself to the ground and seized one of the emptied containers. The dust around it was still moist. Someone, short minutes ago, had broken into this cache and deliberately emptied the water into the dust. Someone....

"Selo!" he half-screamed and staggered to his feet. "Selo," he cried, and remembered his sense of being followed.

Was it the wind among the tortured rocks, or did he hear a high-pitched woman's laugh?

"Selo," he shouted, "I didn't mean to hit you! Selo, you've got to help me!"

Silence.

He began to run.

Exhausted as he was, he must have run for nearly an hour before the unbearable burden of his thirst pushed him down into the granular cushion of the Desert Rouge. A million orange and red parasites clustered on his body and drew out the last drop of his vitality.

Morrissey sighed and stepped closer to the Venusian woman. He felt sure that the clever technicians in Athens would get no story from her.

Two accidental deaths. That would be the verdict.

Morrissey took Selo's arm as she half-stumbled in the shifting dust.

Two men dead—wind-dried mummies fallen in the wastes of the Desert Rouge.

Victims of the desert? Or victims of a woman with deep-set violet eyes and blue-black hair?

Milton Keynes UK
Ingram Content Group UK Ltd.
UKHW030839021124
450589UK00006B/668